THE SCIENCE OF
CRICKET

By
Emilie Dufresne

PLAY
SMART

BookLife
PUBLISHING

©2019
BookLife Publishing
King's Lynn
Norfolk PE30 4LS

ISBN: 978-1-78637-532-2

Written by:
Emilie Dufresne

Edited by:
Kirsty Holmes

Designed by:
Gareth Liddington

CONTENTS

Words that look like **this** can be found in the glossary on page 24.

LET'S PLAY CRICKET

Are you ready to learn all about the **forces**, angles and patterns behind cricket? Then grab your bat and strap on your pads. The match is about to start!

Batters hit the ball and then run between the wickets to score runs.

BATTER

WICKET AND BAILS

FIELDER

Each cricket team has 11 players. Two teams take it in turn to bat, or field. Fielders try to get the batters out by catching balls the batters have hit or knocking the bails from the wicket.

BOWLING BASICS

The aim of bowling is to throw the ball so that it bounces past the batter and hits the wickets. When bowling, it is important to think about speed, **momentum** and angles.

Getting a good run-up before throwing the ball will increase the speed you throw the ball.

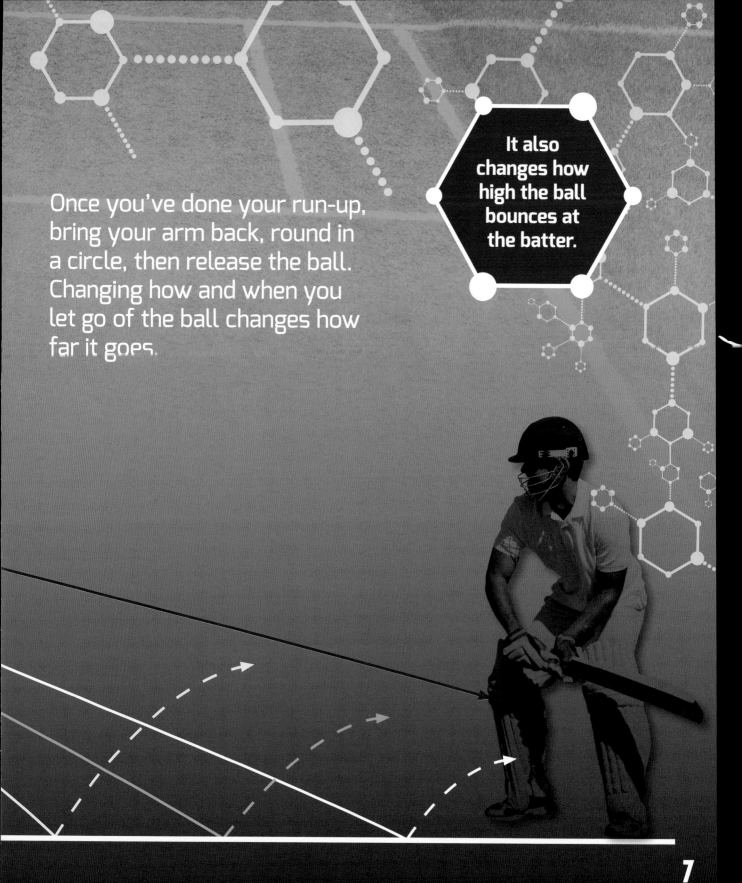

Once you've done your run-up, bring your arm back, round in a circle, then release the ball. Changing how and when you let go of the ball changes how far it goes.

It also changes how high the ball bounces at the batter.

TOP TIPS FOR TOPSPIN

Topspin makes the ball fall to the ground quicker. It also makes the bounce faster and higher than the batter is ready for.

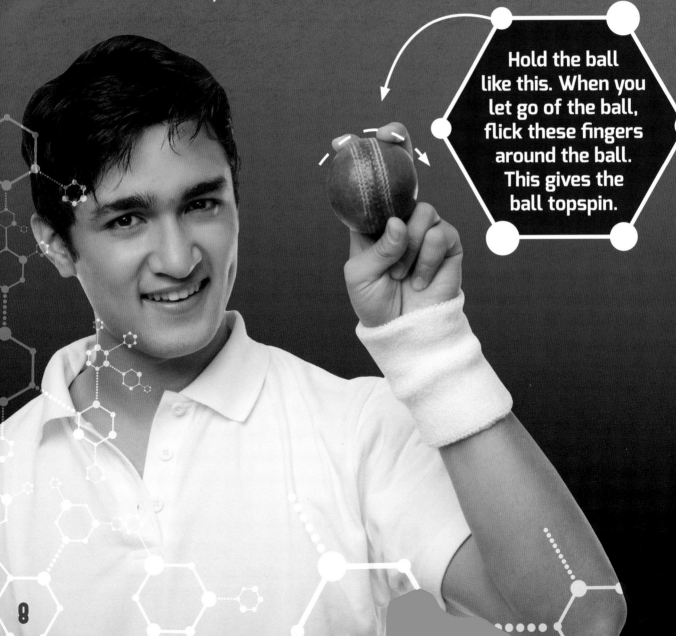

Hold the ball like this. When you let go of the ball, flick these fingers around the ball. This gives the ball topspin.

Topspin creates a forwards and downwards force on the ball. This is because there is higher pressure on top of the ball, which pushes it downwards.

HIGH PRESSURE ←-------

Topspin creates low pressure at the bottom of the ball and high pressure the top.

BALL PUSHED FORWARDS

DIRECTION OF SPIN

LOW PRESSURE

The ball spins faster and in a downwards direction.

BOWL WITH BACKSPIN

Backspin is the opposite of topspin. Instead of **rotating** forwards, it rotates backwards. Twisting your wrist back as you throw the ball will help you do this.

Backspin makes the ball travel a longer distance in the air and land nearer to the batter. Topspin makes the ball travel a shorter distance and land farther away from the batter.

BALL THROWN WITH TOPSPIN

HEIGHT

DISTANCE

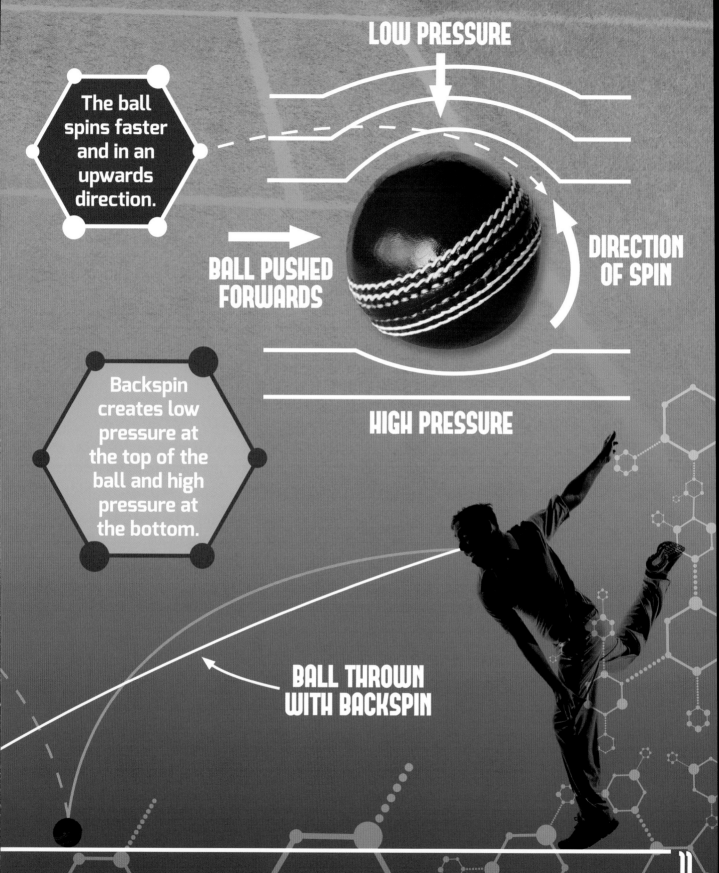

LOW PRESSURE

The ball spins faster and in an upwards direction.

BALL PUSHED FORWARDS

DIRECTION OF SPIN

Backspin creates low pressure at the top of the ball and high pressure at the bottom.

HIGH PRESSURE

BALL THROWN WITH BACKSPIN

BATTING BASICS

When waiting to bat, how you stand is very important.
When waiting for the bowler to bowl, you should stand
with your legs slightly apart so that your body makes
a triangle shape.

HEAD FACING BALL

Keep your knees slightly bent and your head turned towards the direction of the ball, so you're ready to hit.

KNEES BENT

When you get ready to take your shot, pull your bat backwards using your wrists. This is called a back lift.

THE BIGGER
THE ANGLE,
THE HARDER
THE HIT.

THE SMALLER
THE ANGLE,
THE SOFTER
THE HIT.

Swinging
your bat from
different angles
will produce hits
with different
strengths.

THE SWEET SPOT

The sweet spot is on the thickest part of the bat. If the ball hits here, the energy is transferred into the ball, instead of spreading out across the bat.

Hitting the sweet spot means the batter can get the most speed from a hit.

HITTING THE SWEET SPOT GIVES THE MOST EFFICIENT ENERGY TRANSFER.

When you swing the bat, lots of energy and momentum is built up in the bat. When you hit the ball, some of the energy goes into changing the direction the ball is moving in. The rest of the energy is transferred to pushing the ball in the direction of your hit.

MOMENTUM FROM SWING

ENERGY FROM SWING AND THROW TRANSFERRED TO HIT

BALL TRAVELLING IN DIRECTION OF THROW

ON THE DEFENSIVE

For a defensive shot, hold your bat at a 45° angle, facing the ground.

45°

You can play a defensive shot when you think the ball might hit your wickets, or that hitting the ball might get you caught out.

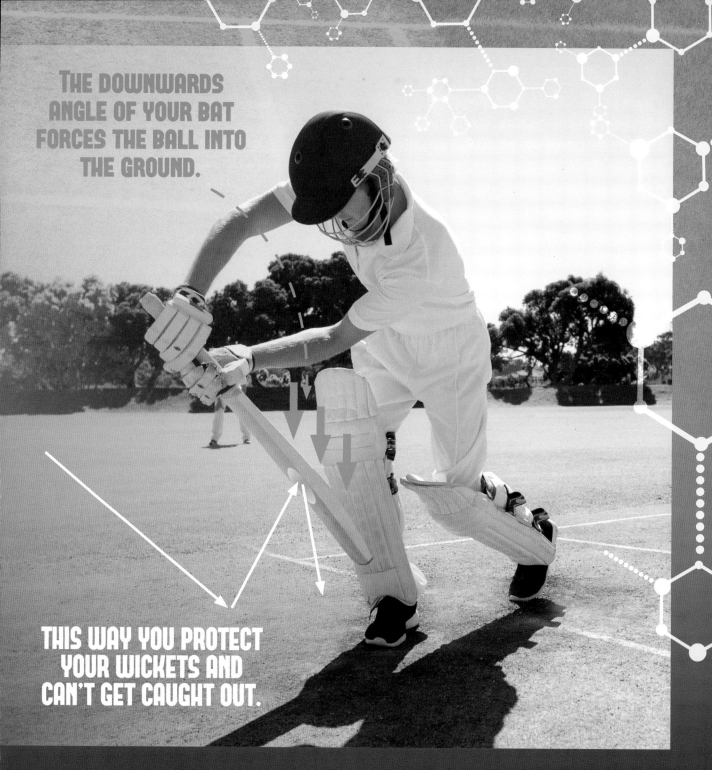

THE DOWNWARDS ANGLE OF YOUR BAT FORCES THE BALL INTO THE GROUND.

THIS WAY YOU PROTECT YOUR WICKETS AND CAN'T GET CAUGHT OUT.

Instead of swinging your bat and creating more force behind the ball, this shot forces the momentum in the ball downwards.

HITTING A SIX

You can score six runs if you hit the ball out of the field. To hit the ball far enough you need to build up lots of momentum in your swing.

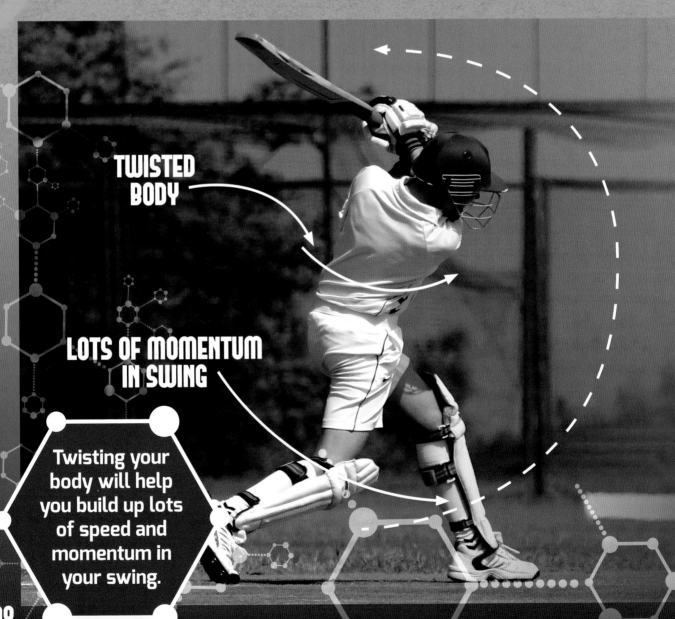

TWISTED BODY

LOTS OF MOMENTUM IN SWING

Twisting your body will help you build up lots of speed and momentum in your swing.

The ball will keep moving in the direction you apply the force.

LIFT YOUR BAT UP HIGH WHEN TWISTING.

DIRECTION OF FORCE

SWING DOWN AND SCOOP THE BALL UPWARDS. FOLLOW THE SWING THROUGH RIGHT AROUND YOUR BODY.

CATCH THEM OUT

To try and catch out the batter, it is important to know the direction, speed and height of the ball. Let's look at this image. How do we know where this ball will go?

THE BALL WILL TRAVEL AT THE SAME ANGLE AS HIS BAT IS HELD.

HIS BODY IS TWISTED SO THE BALL WILL TRAVEL FAR AND FAST.

As a fielder, it's important to know where the ball is most likely to travel. Where do you think the ball is in this picture? Is it number 1, 2, 3 or 4?

Don't forget to think about the angle the bat is being held!

SPOT THE BALL

That's right, it's number 4! Let's take a closer look and see the science behind the shot.

FORCES

The boy has not twisted his body very far, and has not followed through with the shot. Instead of travelling fast and upwards the ball will travel downwards gently.

DIRECTION

The ball will keep travelling in the direction it was hit. We can tell from the twist of the body and the direction of the bat that the ball will travel left.

ANGLES

The bat is angled towards the ground. This means that when the bat hits it, the ball will travel in a downwards direction.

FORCE

DIRECTION

ANGLE

GLOSSARY

defensive	protecting or guarding something
efficient	getting the most out of something in the best way possible
forces	a push or pull on an object
momentum	how fast an object is moving because of its speed and weight
rotating	turning around a central point

INDEX